A SAVAGE TURN

LUKE PATTERSON

This is a Magabala Book

LEADING PUBLISHER OF ABORIGINAL AND
TORRES STRAIT ISLANDER STORYTELLERS.

CHANGING THE WORLD, ONE STORY AT A TIME.

First published 2025
Magabala Books Aboriginal Corporation
1 Bagot Street, Broome, Western Australia
Website: www.magabala.com
Email: sales@magabala.com

Magabala Books receives financial assistance from the Commonwealth Government through Creative Australia, its principal arts investment and advisory body. The State of Western Australia has made an investment in this project through the Department of Local Government, Sport and Cultural Industries.

Magabala Books is Australia's leading independent Aboriginal and Torres Strait Islander publishing house. Magabala Books acknowledges the Traditional Owners of the Country on which we live and work. We recognise the unbroken connection to traditional lands, waters and cultures. Through what we publish, we honour all our Elders, peoples and stories, past, present and future.

Cover design by Jo Hunt
Cover image by Katarina Christenson
Typeset by Post Pre-press Group
Printed by Griffin Press

ISBN 9781922777928 (Print)
ISBN 9781922777942 (ePDF)
ISBN 9781922777959 (EPUB)

A catalogue record for this book is available from the National Library of Australia

Contents

PART 1

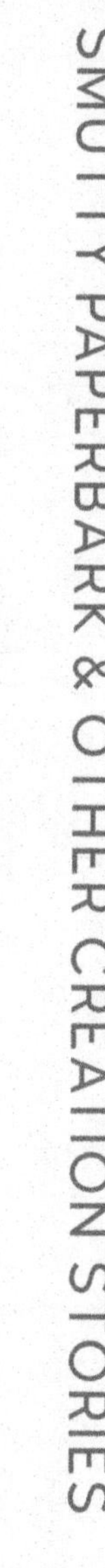

SMUTTY PAPERBARK & OTHER CREATION STORIES

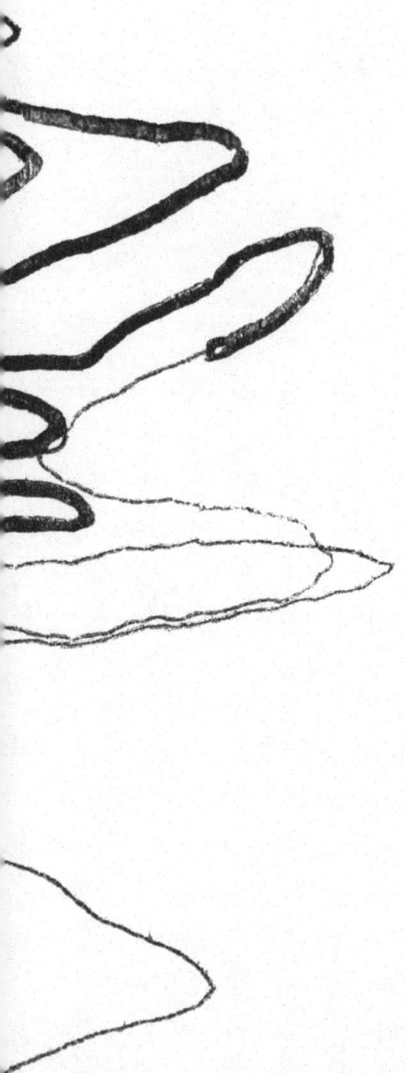

Waratah

You know the way
The story goes

Reading legends
At the flowering stage

Brimstone and blood
Men treading to war

In that dream you have
Grief grows a totem

Like a blown-out
Heart of an emblem

Cleaved
From the ineffable

Creation being
Dying wounded

In the bush
Inflorescence strewn

For the betrayer's
Deadly gift

Australia: A Creation Myth

Before old man cooky
on his boat only darkness,
a fog of warring
savage, a state of nature
for the taking. So they say, so history tells us.

The heavens spun chartless, earth's heathen
children huddled by fire; 'poor creature', the newcomers
thought, approaching the shores of another Eden

to plunder. When old man cooky came on his boat,
two brothers who are now legend, stood sentry
on golden sand and tasted their first musket

shot. The salt air turned foul like earth had opened
its bowels; an explosion signifying
what comes next: a well-oiled machine called colony.

It came and swallowed the birds and their pearls
of laughter heralding sunrise, then shat out
saviours. It came and swallowed

the beasts of the ground, untamed, exalted kin
then shat out the domesticated. It swallowed the trees
mountains and rivers that marked homelands

then shat out houses. It swallowed the flowering
medicines, sweet abundant sustenance, and shat out pox
and profit. It swallowed earth's

custodians, exquisite, ingenious, savage, always savage
but could not consume them.

Ash Lullaby

first rain feeling
in forever folds charred
acacia season
across us–
two stark animals

sooty dark and simmering hills
spit westerly ash
pissy asphalt blooms stink
the land beat black and blue

country whimpers
squandered in a scintilla
hissing industry

what tears a national legend
of supply
chain and heated ire
so swiftly

a spear pierces
the prodigal
settlement stealing stars
from the sky?

as the bullroarer
oblivion
trickles into box-gum
window bushes

of the mind escape

tail end of the boom
earthshaken
us-two
born in burnt-out stump thunder
struck dreaming of coups
wake bellyaching

The Informants

The missionary and linguist asks: 'Little Bird, where is your Country?' Waanytjawaanytja parray ngiruwampa? He parrots the sounds slowly, writes them down in strange orthographies. His first attempt to form the earthly tongue, the word, singing. Talan, wiyelikaane, witiliko. 'Your English is very good.' Ngaba. And Little Bird, interlocutor, whose real name is Kutirun meaning 'flowers on a hill', flew away for ceremony with Old Man Biriban meaning 'eagle-hawk', or who the missionary and linguist calls McGill. And while they were gone, the Man of God cobbled together his words to form *hands, and shoulders, knees and heart*, a grammar: the cudgel and the striker bunkillikan-ne, bunkillikan. He translates them into the Gospel "And you remembered his words" (Luke xxiv: viii) Gatun gaiya bara kotelliela gikoumba wiyelli tara.

Old Man Banksia

here is the wind
that brings life to the flower
cream yellow

chalky cliffs resembling
those of old england

inflorescence bees and honey
honey-eaters perch
antiquities lumpy bark

an opening appearing
like a harbour

this ardent sentry guards
a roughened coast
weathered autochthonous

the appearance
of highest fertility

the flower golden
browns the myth that nature
conspires against us as

our boat proceeded
along the shore

seed in a bunker
wailing for fire singing
for rain elementary

Transit of Venus #1

People will hardly admit
of an excuse
 for a Man leaving
a Coast unexplored
 he has once discovered.

Transit of Venus #2

Impressions of
April 29th, 1770….   Wind southerly and clear
cloudcloth against coast
weather … as we approached the Shore they all made

off, except 2 men, who seem'd resolved to oppose our
Endeavourous
landing … one of them took up a stone and threw, at us,
the white pill placebo sailing Modernity
which caused my firing a Second Musquet, load with

small shott; and altho' some of the Shott struck

the man… advanced into the Woods … we found here
swallow
a few small hutts made of the Bark of Trees, in one of

which were 4 or 5 Small Children, with whom we left
that first myth as
some strings of beads, etc? A quantity of Darts lay
artifactual
about the Hutts; these we took away with us.

Transit of Venus #3

in the Boats in order
During our stay
to row up the Lagoon
in this harbour
we saw a great

deal of smoke
we caused the English
fire
Colours
in a very

small compass
to be display'd ashore
Cockle Shells laying
everyday and an inscription
by them but the

people were gone
to be carved out
they had in the Night
upon one of the Trees
naked as they are

slept in open air.
near

the Watering place …

Eclair Noir (Flash Blak)

I could'a been a little bit French
had La Perouse landed earlier that week
January 26th, 1788.

Men often sail adrift
in search of treasure islands
following faux maps
drawn by sly sailors.

So, I won't speculate too much
about this other no better
or worse à la Australis.

But I like to fathom
I'd be a real flash French Blak.
I'd have a knack for carving croissants
all dreamlike into impossible shapes
like André Breton. He enjoyed
an abstract…

Who knows?
Maybe we'd all be doin' shoeys
out'a Louboutin stilettos
on our national day.

I know it's not right to reduce things down
to black & white like a savage,
signifiers floating nomadically.
But I'm a gap-trapped fulla caught

reading Claude Lévi-Strauss
in the lingua franca: English.

Why don't you listen?
Law written on this peninsula.
You'll have to suffer the misinterpretations.
I'm interested not in what's lost
but what's accrued in cruel translations.

Though I do enjoy feeling the word *'sovereign'*
boom from my feet and out through my throat
because we all know it's about land
and that there are two kinds of people in this world:
those who speak for their own and those who don't.

Rondolettatatat.

Toeing the line
in advance of Austraya fair
is a thin line.
I'm familiar with pale doctrines
and lawless law. The laissez-faire
Ouroboros ride quickly errs
along a line

crash course inline
with its own arse. 'Why should I care
about decline?'
I often wonder. More this 'mine',
'for me', make multi-millionaire
money, feigning unawares
of the deadline.

Misalignment.
The circulatory affair
factory line
of modernity redefines
us-two's relationship and care
of deep sentient ledgers and
ingrained landlines.

We know that line
rehearsed ad infinitum, bare-
thread ghastliness
consumes the future. Reading signs
of Skyfather chroming burnt air,

you, composer in residence,
you know that lie.

Great British Psychodrama

Watch out for the Master's ill
His ill-logic love
His desire to enlighten
The cranial dark of all Otherness

Little Aboriginal boy
Master caucasoid
Will have you
Duped in this fiction
You'll be evicted
To part-time Edens
Full of grief and ill-omens
History haunting a pastoral plot
For a bloody blood continent

He's in your head you see
This affliction
Got you sick in the head
From his criminal cranial renovations
Filled it with a civil story
Of a forgotten then

His purest remnant
Our savage life
Anthropometrically
Funny old hobby
The descent of man for the colony

Headhunting the purest parts

He'll tempt you
Urbane Aborigine the caucasian
Caucasoid master
Savage in master love then absorption
Sees you as his son
Salvaging artefactual fetishisms
Outlandish in your caucasoid body
His property
A fiction man
A man-made wonder
Take on his death mask
What wild white savage
Mongrel mutations mould
Your outlandish caucasoid body
A birthright in concert
With his unlovely love hobby
Safe-ish on this fantastical property
This bloody blood continent
His pastoral graveyard
Master caucasoid's macabre acreage

He's the master of dark arts
Unquenchable lusts
You cut him down
Cut down his heir
His palace
His fair-go
His dreaming
Sickness

Watch out little Aborigine
Little pale picaninny

If you're not careful
He'll make you
Make you his
His figurehead
His domesticated
No more law-scars no more boomerang
Just breastplate certificate
Charge by the dot

Be one of his minister
Of the cross or the cabinet
Strive to the highest
Office in the land
And rule as a quantumised priest-king
His kingdom in middle class ruin
In fractured fractions
In his savage lawless lock
The country cracks beneath us

A split consciousness
Victim and prize
Curiosities Resurrected
Renewable indifference

Can you sing between his lies?
Our bones
Our blood
Our lands
Our Seas
Our skies
Breath in the living history
The little world beyond

Lilli-pilli fields
Where you emerge strong
Adorned in seasonal language
And nakedness
Seasonal love
As legend tells us

In a Name

Light-bringer, wielder
of the wooden sword, made
of wood, from the battle-
ground, he who knits dark
between the stars, deep water,
spook, skywalker, father's son,
strangers tell me they're my father
but dad lives sustainably an hour
outside of Rockhampton,
I'm nobody too.

A Great Australian Adjective

Absobloodylutely
It's a bloody blood oath
Bloody no treaty bloody hell bloody
Bloody lucky country
Bloody sunday bloody sunday
I don't bloody think so
Blood orange
Blood bank

River's bloody blood hound
Bloody pore
Bloody beautiful
Where the bloody hell are you

Bloody lovely day
Bloody rains
Bloody kids
The bloody missus

Bloody fantastic
You bloody ripper
My bloody word
A bloody mission
A bloody admission

Someone threw the bloody rubbish out

The roads are a bloody mess
Bloody waters everywhere

Bloody river is flooded

Go on for bloody ever
back to bloody bumfuck nowhere

Gorgeous bloody view
Fan-bloody-tastic
blood money

Dead as a bloody pose
Blind as a bloody bat

Urgent bloody blood delivery

Bloody coincidence

Bloody ridiculous

Bloody blood feud

The bloody baby took my dingo
Aunt said it wasn't appropriate
to have in this poem

Bloody pisshead
On the bloody piss
Old bloody pipe

Bloody dickhead
Bloody murder

Punctuated punctured bloody fuck fuck

Primal Aches

There is a wayward crow
that I think

discovered cruelty
terrorising the dead

end street magpies
and lorikeets by breaking

their wings in a series
of pecks and taunts

warbles gobbled
in chortles before

the noisy miner's
cop formations herd

the black one off
I race to the epoch holding

a bundi cudgel carved
to beat the demons off and

I'm wearing boxershorts and grey
oversized longsleeve T grandma

picked up on sale with 'Forever
Fearless' bordering a tiger's

portrait passing as ridiculous
and I'm singing "Fuck Off Circle

of Life (never trust a man
who claims to be king)"

but I'm too late for the magpie
pup limping around the front lawn

this fucking currawong curating
on the wire right about my head

indifferent to this too-late-again-
aborigine who went on to write

a poem about the end of the
world and I had to let it go

Smutty Paperbark – A Post Colonial

I drop the blak
like a culture bomb.
Dancing possum,
waltzing ghostgum.
A figment of the left
of centre and just right
for development.

A policy success,
I wear all the native brands.
Aboriginal. Indigenous.
Descended, identified, accepted.
From the beginning. Belonging
to the land. Neither here nor now.
Somewhere outside of time
but firmly in my place.
Since time immemorial, and
according to science
for 60 0 0 0 ish yea rs.

In other words, I assume
the missionised position
and learn to hate
my face spread-eagle
with a smile, yes boss.
Call my land
line a bluff, go on.
Play pin the phenotype
on the mongrel.

I am a dot-painting on a dunny-roll,
an acrylic fable, a smutty
paperbark novel.

I drop the blak
like a culture bomb.
The market is good
for fair skin fullas with half
a brain and a whole lot
of dumb luck.
Though still
unsure whether
to mention on résumé
Aboriginal and/or Torres Strait
Islander when applying
for non-identified jobs.

You want me to be
the digestible kind of blak
Your Mulatto Sonata.
Good for acknowledging country
and facilitating cultural
competency afternoons,
revamping your reconciliation
action plans, charming
old white ladies to donate to your cause.

Because
I'm articulate as a snowflake
though not nearly original
dropping the blak
like a culture bomb.

Collecting bits of broken china
in a coolamon.
Every second shard
has dreaming in the title.
They're adequate facsimiles
with romantic watermarks.

You want me to translate well on page
and frame conversations carefully
when I say gubba whitefulla wadjin
I'm your parade,
pedigree prince
familiar with the eye
that plays tricks.

More or less unmarked
I'll pose like a question
swimming butterfly against the tide
of history.
Hiding the trauma.
Hiding the shame.

I'm Blackapedia,
as british as tea.
I thought I was black
jesus with a secret/sacred
constellation of freckles speckled
on my arse
but then the southern cross
became a symbol for bashing
people of colour.

I drop the blak
like a culture bomb.
Sex the lyrebird and raze the city
with a chainsaw song.
Strum the mandolin
to soothe my grandmother's
nerves mastering the master's
hands and listening to elders chant
an ancient harangue tone-throwing
to the cosmic intelligent,
slapping us all in the face
like a Murray-Darling
dead perch bog.

I drop the blak
like a culture bomb
to piss off pundits like Akerman
and Bolt. Spark fire in my belly and eyes.
Make me wild. Make me sharpen
the tongue. I fantasise of a faceoff
in kangaroo court systematically dismantling
their barely veiled ethnocidal tendencies
in the one hand, the other holds
a spear aimed for the leg.
The nation will shed crocodile tears
in memory of free speech.
I'll be accused of living
that dark underbelly,
dark unspoken secret that fills the telegraph
and sunrise tv every other everyday. That naturalised
violence. That somehow Aboriginal = Disease.
Go on, Bring on the tanks!

I drop the blak
like a culture bomb.
I wear my black,
yellow, red even though
I'm growing more
and more apprehensive of ethnic
nationalism.
I wear my scales, furs
and feathers. Freshwater.
Saltwater. Red dirt black dirt.
Beachside. Bushside.
A streak of volatile ochre
across my forehead.
Even though I'm growing
more and more skeptical of
philanthropic blak
excellence.

I'm no weak coffee.
I'm a wild willy-wag.
A silly-billy-dilly-bag
Trying to hunt down the min-min, Me! Me!
Cheeky buggers
I saw dance. Deadly!
Lithe bodies leaping over the
silhouette tress of far off mulga.
White sugary stuff, late October.

I am an allegory.
An anti-colonial killjoy.
An SJW carrying on.
Just identity politics. Poetics

and polemics. A greedy socialist, fascist, capitalist,
feminist, activist, queer-ass scumball.
I'm so infamous you thought I was dead.
Sucked in! I'm Captain Crook, the first Australian
and your first Blak PM.

But why get even when I can get it all?
Climbing the ladder of so-called blak benefits
with my so-called
free Toyota.
Free education.
Free home loan.
Free prescriptions.
Free premature death-sentence.
Free benevolent hand.
Free ride on the gravy train to concessions
and successions.
Give back the land!

I drop the blak like a culture bomb because
today is not the day for polite or tight poems.
I am a messy text. I am out of control.
When words fail I reserve the right to scream
And play Settlers of Catan with a ruthless eye
for your land and one day own a small
quad bike business ripping up the sand
on the dunes of a sorry place. That's my sick
irony. I survive on imperial violence.
What percentage am I white? What genealogy must weep?
Grey lights, a knife, a subincision
to extract those sleep beings of Gondwanaland.
I am skinned.

If I lose and live I'll eat flash devon, and do the bro-shake
with my brothers in our lap-lap suits.
And if not, if I win, bury me in a tree on heritage listed land.
Just one more up-yours, carving clubs and boomerangs
in the bellows of another generation.
I am a problem. Always was, Always will be.

Invasion Eve

January 25th, sitting in a Redfern park.
Abundance of fallen leaves thick with resin moisture
enough to convey the idea of animals slaughtered
under branches. I'm dissociating, dissolving
in the birds-eye glamour: the earth is an abstract painting.
I'm not thinking about dates or what season blood runs
through sap. I'm just trying to catch the sunlight,
write about unoccupied seasonal events, calling it
eco-poetry to pay the rent.

Redfern crows mock
the endeavour. All the lines
contain spirits of the dead and audiences
are advised hurt carries across generations.
I'm worried all my poems should contain
trigger warnings and spithoods.

I go back to writing my poem,
'January 25', the one I've been writing since the day
before invasion. I intend to read it
over the weekend. in my mind's eye,
I'm accompanied by the hottest 100 massacres
and dance shake-a-leg better than I actually can.
It's about survivor's guilt
and gammon community consultations.

Off Country

I don't know the dreaming
of this terrain

only languages bled in
from sandstone

boulder country west
and east running the salt

water people escape
measly heat itching

for a healing place
as government men

unconcerned with God
passed for greener pastures

Mountain Ash

all the gums are haunted now
old growth

timber shedding
ribboned bark

like spirits
spilled across a canvas

Three Sisters

medicine man
lost his bone
no culture hero

just sisters
turned to stone
take a photo

PART 2

A SAVAGE TURN & OTHER LOVE SONGS

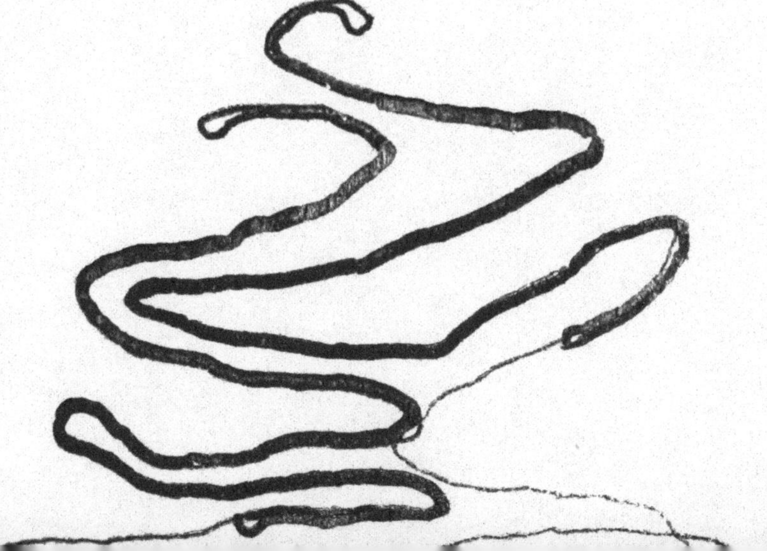

To What Earth We're Heir

I see you bub
covered in bruises and cuts
wrestling with angels
who are demons
protectors who are keepers

I know self-loathing
sails in from time to time
as you try to catch
echoes try to catch air

and the strange estrangement
bloodletting a trail
of birth certificates
a trail of death
certificates

no trace
of birth or death
but a mention
on mission registers
unspeakable skeletons
defleshed in the closets
of godfearing forefathers
spreading the good word
across this burnt continent

it is what it is
to live another day

with the blak slapped out of us
with white whispers
telling you to host dirty little secrets
we were bred to fester
in our heart
shoot us for dead
then absorption
convince us to forget
who we are

bear the wound hard
clear-headed
full of fire my love
unlearn the master's mantra
learn what happened
here to whom

bleed for scar trees
expose your vulnerability
your mask uncoming done
I'll hold you

because true-god our truth
hurts it burns to the last
embers of your life
but it's worth it if you're willing
to let the lucky country die

and in that death
you'll find
wattle flood the street
we engender our own bodies

take care of the weak
without worrying
about survival
our birthright

yes bub
the day will come
when we claim
what earth we're heir
and holiday on country
on the ruins of parliament house
and our ancestors sleep sound
home in skycamp

The Cooee That Comes Back to You

us-two appear
shell skinned in delicate spring
all cheek chill nip and salt bitten

attuned to the tideline's sheer
wash and correspondence
sublimated under a waratah sunrise
nudie naturalis

we are droplets
kissed being kissed
kissed
by

us
-two
be
come
a rush
of hot air
cool air skin
hand hair mixed
mythologies and pigments

our fingers tangle
untangling deep time
inscriptions odorous
emphatic rhythms of kelp
and deconstructed mollusc

self-organised cellular
refractions micro-lithic
carbon kingdoms

we find our feet
and collide in the first
ow or oh or oo the first
word the first cooing
and cooee
that comes back
to you

a tumble of laughter
and pipi stories spun
within our grandmothers

and the old fullas
whose faces resemble
the trace of mouth
and brackish lip
not a line but a circuit
articulating remarkable
formations connecting coast
and mountain through sea
eagle eyes soaring awesome

as all love spirals here
in autochthonous breaths
us-two walk this track
along the shore upriver to the core
and return a thousand lifetimes

lace dry dune grass
on oyster rock
set fire to the smokey manna stuff
sipping rainstorms
from the other country

A Grass Tree by Any Other Name

Flora and fauna have taken over the apartment.
We come together spreading like wildfire, like rain.
Not the country we had hoped–three flights high
on stolen land–but it's our slow-growing peace
for when we tire of the Australiana dreamtime.
A place we can hang our emu feather earrings,
wash ochres from each other's skin, leave our keys
in a coolamon carved from the knee of a river red,
without white superstition or political subtext.
Spectacles recede into the chirping suburban buzz
and flushed by an ancient patience, green thumb,
I watch your hedge magic season our landscape
In wetness opalescent as crocodile tears. Almost
lyrical the way you spin leaf and afternoon light.
A ceremony taking your time tending the grass
tree, potted knee-high, stump burnt black, stem
sun-soaked and sprouting past our heads. Flowering
names we keep a secret. This bush love sacred.

Our Poetica

I'm telling a lover
about poets and their thing
for red wheelbarrows.

They knows me
long enough
to get it. We listen

to Barton's didge
and orchestra
from our new speakers.

Rain trundling
against the window.
Feels like we're in

a Frank O'Hara poem
stirring wattle seed
pancakes for dinner.

Transit of Venus #4

They again visited the Sound.
Being on board, I went immediately ashore,
There were 6 Canoes,

variable light airs, and calms, in the night, the 6
I follow'd alone and unarm'd some distance,

small fires had a light breeze from the land,
they would not stop until they went further off than
muscles roasting on the fires, some oysters
I chose to trust myself, and disappeared
laying there; We tasted of their Cheer
armed in the same manner

and we left them in return
as those that came yesterday.

Transit of Venus #5

I went in the pinnace to the head
in order to Examine the Country, and
to try to form Connection.
We found the face of the Country much
the same as I have before described, but the
land much richer for instead of Sand
I found in many places a deep black
soil, which we thought was Capable of
producing any kind of grain; and
Timber, as fine Meadow as ever was
seen; however, we found it not all like
this, some few places were very rocky,
but this, I believe, to be uncommon. The
stone is sandy, proper for building, etc.

Transit of Venus #6

Saw the Island, by variations   that Breeze
of the compass. Noon anchored   perpendicular to Actual Measure-
at the Buoy,   ment I kept sometime Longer.
Log and Observed.   This morning Sun and Moon
Found our Selves   Served Portable Soup
in Squalls,   squealing with thunder.

Letter of the Land

you've given me a new name
in a dead language
air-dried and light-eaten by history
flattened the colour gone
pressed to the page
stored and studied
facsimile after facsimile

you so admired
the first razor leaf with cream covered
flowers flush pink red and the plumb darker side
of austral bracken possibilities
you chose stasis
left your indifference
in climate controlled coffins
absent uncirculating

unable to sing without returning
to regenerate to nourish to burn
I am an artifice and fact of thieves
found along the margins of rivers
and creeks where I ponder
your garden culture and self-imposed
enclosure written in the mundane
avenue woodlot windbreak and park

you have tasted my berries
acid sweet when ripe
without a thought for the seasons

you feel heartburn belly ache
and in this restless sleep you ghostwrite
dreams on tattered paperbarks

I have said my peace with ghostly whims
and forget-me-all oils pirated from tea-tree
ornamental

yielding
I have taken
in your bowery and bleeding hearts
said my peace with your intrusions
the silence in your sciences
where at the sterile apex tip
a black-ish stigma
taxonomic name not included

no matter how you try to own
to possess my expanse and breadth
remember that I hold
you within my arms
and now my children come knocking
to retrieve the particles of me stolen
in so-called good faith

don't be surprised when I rise
teaching again the first great archive
reigning all over you

Breaks

breaking open
torpor sleeping they say
like snow country
no country sleeps anymore
too hot

but some very clever people
left knots in the lexicons
for us to find

Salt

honour to dance
this tidda's song

sea-her become song
woman calling

across five islands
to worimi

signals I swim
the peripheries

as bubs
acquire knowledge

their shapeshifting
murmuration bubbles

become whale
become dolphin

self-regulating
orchestration

breaching sea-sky
country spilling over

what it's like to be
on the other side

of here, on our way
home to water

Black Arts

Inspired by Karla Dickens' installation *A Dickensian Circus* at the Art Gallery of NSW

Exhibit A.

off-white busts
of old men watch on

a rusty red vintage
fetish for the fanatics

memory and myth mixed
phenotypes for pleasure

min-min are the jailer's invention
they crawled out a cage

see em dancing
to the survivalist jig

hear em singing in the bloody
bora circus ring

in the heart of a paddock
lines of fences slicing

the land
blood on the hands

when the dust clears
a museum settles

an alcove lined with
feathers canvas classics

love magic lingers
take a peek behind the curtain

a sideshow has petrified
these settler sins

Exhibit B.

where is your companion
you look subdued in your hushed hessian
sweet tooth black cockatoo
have the floors been scrubbed
the linen lugged and pegged
payment suspended
your face rendered national talisman
you pull a cheeky grin sharp as lightning
and a storm approaches
your brood is mourning
by fire in the distance
a curse on those who have come
to circumnavigate you
pay attention to these explorers
plumbing the depths
they'll put your likeness
on enamelled tins on a pedestal

and call it wholesome
a mission bub loved
living in a humpy
made of matchsticks

Exhibit C.

lord hung the piccaninni angels
in the asylums of heaven
made them parade
their wares and wings

pray bird, what are you?
                                swallow
                                willy wag
                                pidgin
                                wedge
                                sparrow
                                galah
                                whatever you need to be

the metal is seasonal
they recycle pain
here in god's country
and the hounds
dumb drunk on cherub tears bark
            at the border of humanity
            order by cloth and cross and crown
your sanity locked up
and somehow
the devil lives upside down

like a bat
in your head all along
offering solace

you set off in a dream
twilight flying free
dim ember sun
over the blackened horizon
eating fruit and bugs
like a true god
weaving the last stars into tropes
that pull the world on
as a dilly full of story

Ciggies and Bleach

My grandma and sister
smoking ciggies and bleaching floors.
They're helping me move into the cul de sac home
I bought with my partner in dreaming.
My grandma and sister's gossip echoes
soft as emu feathers and love letters
in the empty space, sweeping
shadows from the skirting boards,
exiling ghosts from the kitchen cupboards.
My grandma and sister
doing an emu dance like we did as kids, dhinawan
teaching us to pick up the pieces of our past.
Grandma swears every time she quits smoking
one of her kids dies. I let her get away
with it because it's true and Mum's the only one left.
We have our superstitions, shit that haunts us.
My grandmother is of that generation
where clean house and holy mouth might stop 'em
from taking your kids away.
And me? I subtract my age from that of my uncles
when they died, even though I don't want to
be a poet prophet. It's better now
except my sister says post-referendum
the nephews and nieces are bullied at school,
told they'll be sent away. We couldn't figure out where.
But everything is ok because Grandma and sister
are conducting cultural business

with ciggies and bleach
as I help carry pot plants to the courtyard
with my partner in dreaming.

Darkinjung Burning

begin with a circle facing a fire aunty
lit under the blinking pink and kindle
dawn moon nevertheless splashing
in the breeze rest handfuls of striplet
sprigs moiety-up arc an interspecies
intimacy until a dozen landscapes egress
with a eucalyptus lungful and the supernatural
appear commonsense in tempered embers
this is not a mourning poem you see
places are totemic uncle dips bottlebrush
dew admits life begins with yellowbelly
untroubled chuckle in gestures
the way the land-owner cites edible plants
surveys the shape the colour of eyes
a course of native spices peppers cosmopolitan
phenotypes he smokes a pipe with a timber
pulse and jokes how he plundered through
dark emu in a week thanks god for the
seasons urging to get on with business
eat biscuits wait for the wind to calm
sheepish hawks circle thermal pockets
birdsong warms the valley lips aunty
calls a tenure of love a labour of warmth for light
for ceremony for hardening the point spearhead
the facts face the leviathan that gags
the undergrowth and wraps its brambled body
around the roots untouched scales a forsaken
gallery this toothache country uncle growls years
of gub-abo leaf litter over his old shoulders

letting in a little peace of sky country
the air which left untended is prone to ignition
aunty yawns two-stepping with a willy wagtail
drip torch in her hand tilts yolk from an egg
little min-min ooze out dance fiddle-footed
nothing cataclysmic no holocenic genocide
no pyretic extinction just a fizz seeds pop tickle
lick with a pitch and chimerical taste of species
in cahoots no war but a wash of living soot no
breakneck rush but simply slips down the slope
flush like a droplet down the wrist a chittering
of carapaces and critters scurrying up trunks
a breath before a din no woodwind lakestorm
no brouhaha only the heartstrings the burning
diphthong unbuttoning years of flora and flesh
lost in language we walk and talk on a hotbed
rolling bio-semiosis side-by-side a wandering
phantonym in mnemonic attires cool to the touch
and calm as wallabies watching in the distance

Who is the Sun?

You are the sun
Who asked for nothing.
And I keep on growing.
And we keep on growing.

Double Brick Aspirational

late september sunday afternoon
eucalyptus blossom
roast lamb in the air
open the side gate
smothered with heraldic wattle

passing through the sunlit
thick yellow
mottled in lorikeet hues and laughter
sis sings

whole-hearted welcomes
with niece in arm
and swapping bub for apple crumble
she lands a kiss and nips
off for a well-deserved rest

on uncle duties I follow
sovereign footsteps
across the yard path
and the colours of my day
are complete as I spot

mighty defenders, wild
nephews dressed as proud pirates
constructing humpies from hard-rubbish
our black-yellow-reds flying
an insurgence of love above

and before us with us
watching from the garden's heartland
covered head-to-toe in mud
nightgown and full makeup on
grandma exudes a deep-time elegance

humming her sweet sundown music
amongst veggies
suspiciously strong
a ritual increase a flowering
synonymous with poetry

front and back this flash Gadigal
hill-top double brick dream home
so far from her fibro beginnings
where now in the twilight hours
of a tired nation

I invoke the old art
of making fire
and plot tender revolutions
with the future custodians
of our little grassroots empire

Data Fields

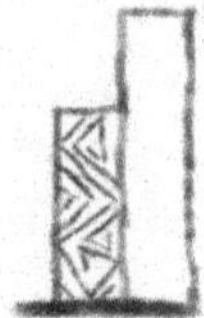

Once upon a bleep in our history
Against the concrete

Melaleuca quietness
Matter of factly a necropolitics set in

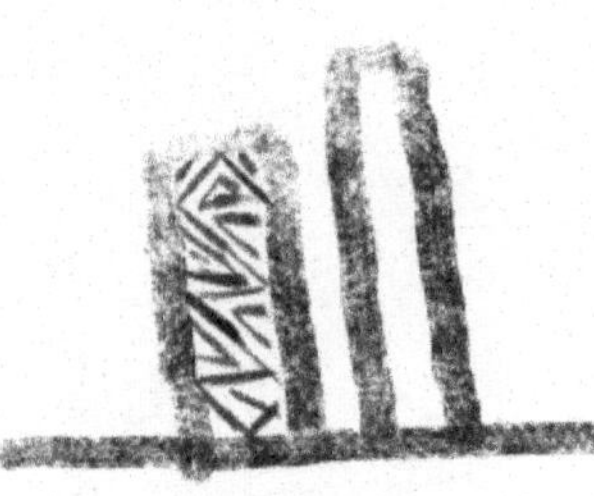

Living in a gap
The shadowiness the ugliness that is

Ghost-hunting for uncles and aunties
Fearful of the their footsteps

Six feet deep
Living in the gap has got me anxious

Within the rising Bulwark
Statistical-scar trees of modernity

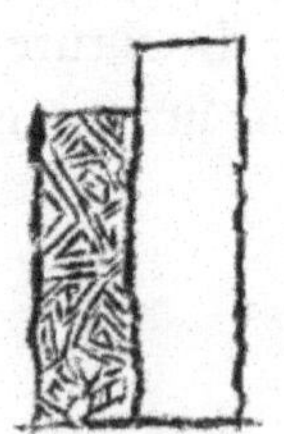

This burial ground I have wondered in on
Casts shadows solid growing as an oil spill

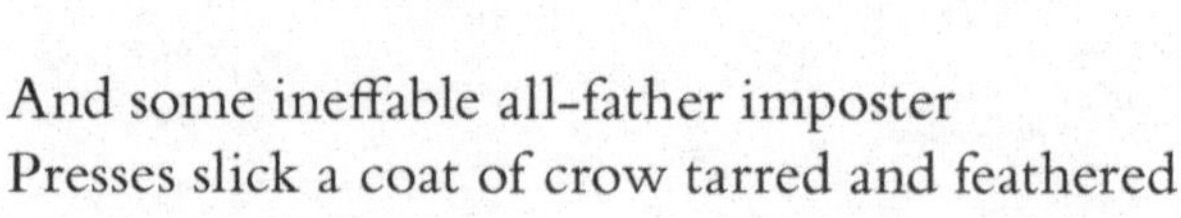

And some ineffable all-father imposter
Presses slick a coat of crow tarred and feathered

My flesh made intelligibly deficit.

A Savage Turn

This is the poem
where I'm meant to spill my guts and you read the entrails
where I talk further about deceased uncles and aunties
who bought me barbies and taught me karate respectively
and it's that poem I've been writing for years
this is the poem that was meant to be all
titular dead centre where I solve and sell trauma
I seriously thought I could convince you of treaty with tricks
I began with a broken promise
promising specifics and the right imagery
this is the poem that I vial
plant medicine and anti-venom
made and in-making
I haven't surrended yet
the poem
of calling myself a modern savage
writing my name in the sand
then for some reason spitting on it
to give it a good polish
I was meant to cave in
to anthropology and confession
not like bloodletting but I wouldn't know anyway
this is the poem lodged amongst the love
poems just a scattering
and all sedition
this poem was the aha! moment
it was meant to make sense of everything
and I promise to add it to my next collection
if we live that long.

Curlew

Nocturnal. We are
biology under light of moon
and summoner of storm.
We prefer to walk.

Cryptic.
Our appearance alludes.
We are fallen timber.
We are grass.

We are leaf litter chromatics.
Thick-kneed. Stilt-legs.
Large head. Yellow eyes.
Our song is fear

in timbre. We play the wailing
infant. The mourning mother.
Our chorus raised on sex.
We are massacre

by the river. Hisses. Clicks.
Croons. A coda
of shuddering plume.
Bringers

of grave news. Unfettered.
We. Dream. Appear.
Unsettling.

Dreaming Inside Dillwynia Women's Prison

To the external world
The philosophy of nature
We are all animals
And she is the sacrificial

I didn't know the cat's mother
Or her totem's name
Or what she did
Or what she does at lockdown 3pm

Aunty doing a life's lag
Maps the room and all
Our blood relations
All bearers, human & bestial

Tiddas

So much taken from you
through tricks and shapeshifting.
It's the oldest story in the sky
but the world won't listen.

Under Wiradjuri Sky

Somewhere under Wiradjuri sun,
out of the way
the sky takes on a sharper blue
through razor wire.
There are lines humming
here still, you know. Strange,
blunt thuds, lock after lock.
In the hallway the muffled
intercom buzz. Disarming.
Scanned, checked, finger printed.
Identity disassembled
(intentionally?)
This visitor's lanyard around my neck
and the light wanes to an institutional white.

After Big Rain

Floodplain fat with sky,
no beginning or end

to the 'Bidgee stretch.
A circle story swirling

the stuff of legend.
Aunt recites a lesson

homeward, rippling out
from the old station

town with its haunted
house, confectionary &

correctional facilities.
The boot is full

with precious *Dreaming*
Inside stories, volatile

knowledge exposing
the bloodier history &

how prisons are marvels
of social engineering.

UnLoreful

The law calls him

An adult a bad guy

He's created victims

Been one himself

Ruled out for

Safe Keeping

Deficit

A punitive turn

Cracking his head

Against a wall

Of legal fictions

Committed to

Prejudice

Housebroken

With a stern warning

Aboriginal child

With no priors

Cento – They come to our house [1]

Where nan was our home
Different nations tellin
Storys with our hands
Longest living culture
That Dreamtime serpent fire
Place you come from
The lifestyle you want
You can be anything

Then taken off your land
Must be the government's plan
You needed money to live
Always doing 'big boy' things
Backpack full of trauma
You are who you hand around
On an earn run amok
Watch your back
You had to learn
You got given back to the system
Place of steel
Timed phone calls
Talking about what you'll do after

3 months
7 months
in and out
6 years
8 years

Long time in custody
Criminally labelled
Things you been through and done
Looking beyond, beyond

And when you're old enough
To get a job and feel the fresh air
Against your face down mystery bay
Where unc' plays guitar and we sing
Along, speak, it's from the chest
Weapon sunsets

Flow like your home river
Forever changing, maturing, getting older
Understanding trauma (I can't explain)
Learn traditional and new way
Going from estate to estate
From Dubvegas, BrisbaneBronx
to Alcheringa

---

1 Lines from this poem are drawn from *Scribbly Gums and Blossoms: Young People Dreaming Inside*, an anthology developed through the Ngana Barangarai program.

PART 3

THE OTHER SIDE OF COUNTRY

Kurnell

lined with norfolk-pining nostalgia-thin
myths of peaceful settlement I'm wondering
why I return to your history strung out

in clay-bone-coloured coastal rhythms—
kurnell seaside hometown crooning 250
years on I've come tumbling back to you

and your glittering intellects of old dreamings
known best with eyes and creased brow
unfolding into colossal lecturers of silence

and listening to the hours graze against
your cliff face back to ocean universities—
country that built my head and heart

a country shrunk and rose in gold dunes
and sunk again under the weight of caltex
tycoon sewage plants and sand mines

speed-sweeping the solemn hills for progress
theft heaving in its wake a crest of unaffordable
beachside deco-chic shacks and nautical

themed mcmansions anchored on display—
it's a flagworld day in the complacent now
a flag to conquer and/or be conquered

in these land-grabbing games descended from

james these blind inventions and life-size
replicas of life detailing the way museums

and mausoleums help us to forget
the crown that burns off empires of waste—
kurnell you harbour my mad longing to see

the milky way arc its dewy star-stained net
dip in the river of night where earth and sky
reflect impossible symmetries so

I walk midthought head-high among the wild
flannel flowers thirsty drink from a stream
time has carried my freshwater blood in one

great maternal canoe and one great paternal
canoe drifting from the north and northwest
along past wheat fields grain silo opal extractions

and folks fracking for redemption all the way
here to the land of the tharawal to tharawal
lands where I am the sum of black dirt

and red dirt mob holding on to barefoot knowledge
and ancestral accents old pondering songs I keep
close to defend against the spoon-fed grey-tamed

answers of domesticated curlews
and dust worshippers whose poverty of love
ring in the end of time with a ka-ching

to the invention of exteriority

in the margins of intimacy our footsteps tread lucid
as light through the half open eye-lid & beyond
each corner is an abbreviature a blueprint out
of the shadows in which we brush up on our trust test
courage find love in the undiscoverable
Country

announce here a telltale & homespun
view memories aired & mementos sown as
honeyed phrases somatic amendments floating their
way through the ear & like cloudscapes above the
salted horizon our freelance thoughts breast into clear cut
pluralities
held cradled nourished

the land remembers the shifting coastals mending
broken stories of a shaken epoch & in the cool
alertness
in dew time daylight flowers we offer a piece of
ourselves offer space to the undulatory shapes
of settlement
we remember the names woven here these
entanglements as they cast an ocean over
our shoulders & in the buttery afterthought
our visions return us

to the invention of interiority

Salt Water Painting

I know a fulla, who knows a crane, who knows a gull. Intimately.
He tells me to be careful the way you tell another's story. Be
Careful the way you reframe, snapshot, screenshot, turn pigment
Into pixel into poem. That fulla worries when I snoop other mob's
Warnings. Whorled into their sweet lullabies, entranced, indulging
In the distant textures of land, sea, sky. I reach out to touch scars
Of an islandology not my own. And, wonder how actions harden
To engender the body. Not everything is fixed like a fingerprint, so
I begin focussing on the motions, the making, the winds, the breath,
The spirit. You know, that flow, shaping our closeness to Country.
Held in tow by the yarns of my own mob, I let go of the picturesque
As the requisite for meaningful growth. I try making connections.

River Red

once upon an old bush liar's song
born in burly bark huts and outback gothics
baulk balladeers throw offcuts to mongrel
dingo pups stolen from blackfulla camp

yonder. here where the river red tilts
to meet dark water you'll see their ghostly
shreds entangled in twisting branches.
all the gums haunted now and the billy can
boils curse after curse cut from the crust
of land they did not know or bother to love.

these bush poets spun slack lined verses
ear-worming deep into the heartwood
though they never tasted true sustenance
songmen without spirit without substance

Untitled

I'm not even sure
how to speak

my father's Country
or tame the river

dog's cunning drag
to the bog bottom

of reconciliation.
But I tell nieces &

nephews to remember
the way fire gives

space to meaning,
how to blend voiced

& voiceless wattle ash
for the old people

sunrise to sunset. I tell
'em everything a story.

Triolet x2

Aunt points to the lagoon
where she was born.
The mud is thick, insects hoon
as aunt shows me her lagoon
The sun sets and even the moon
is listening to a story born.
Aunt is the lagoon
where she was born.

|

Between layers of silver bark
moth larvae trace
zigzags and circuitous arcs.
between layers of silvery bark
a caterpillar feasts on scar
tissue. In the hidden place
between layers of silvery bark
a moth emerges moon faced.

Parable

Uncle David slayed
Goliath and the government
backed off.

'That's mamma
leaning through the humpy
window.' The plaque

named Aboriginal
Place after the amusement
park and racecar club went

into dissolution. He said
They made the land beautiful
again. Some apple

trees were left
reminding the old aunts
of hessian sacks for dresses

and not much to eat
but fruit in the gully.

Aboriginal Owned

at the cultural centre
a woman's law stick

hanging on the wall
nudges gravity loose

signifying we mean
business and that

this house of myth
ain't for fools

we see cross thatched
patterns of exchange

Arnhem ochre flaking
familiar names

weapon-tools worth
as much as the ute

(a thing of legend
in itself) and stories

stories driven here from
out Wiradjuri way

we delight in the deadly
taxidermy collection

a possum a wallaby
a feral cat froze bung

we keep looking
for that souvenir shop

acrylic imported
didge and roo scrotum

the row of boomerangs
all exactly alike but

not even an ornamental
spoon to bring home for nan

Night Vision

Beyond the eyelid's flickering light, strange
how you teeter. Marsh frogs in their homes shake
the shallow waters of these hours. Their song
across space naked spills through an opened window.

Here, in this half-sleep dulcet rhythm, lifted,
your mind drifts along currents patterned by gentle
moth wing flutters. Everything abuzz, you float,
dance, fathom amongst sweet-lipped night flowers.

Colourful quiet, at furthest point from day, the stars
brighten, blanketing. A sugar glider slides down
a moonbeam to gnaw and sip on summer softened
fruit, radiant wattle nectars. You nestle, cozy

within a nook-hollow of the great river red gum,
swaying, protected by the boobook owl. Tender hoots
remind you of the vastness connecting earth and sky.
The whole circus hooped within you, dreamer.

Portant

On the spoil-heaps of mines and quarries
I sing even when all the flowers have gone.
I walk around leaking feathers, attempting
to see through bird eyes, old stories curled
within stone to conjure voices rattling like teeth
or loose change, they echo from the bottom
of the savage spirit's realm where ancestors
famously home from …   slip along
thick pulses of light. A spider weaves intricate
threads. There I hang, about to be eaten
by the black one.

A Lizard (Shot on iPhone)

You were dormant and now the water
dragon, unflinching on a white rock—

It's Dharug today, but tomorrow's Gumbanggir
will give another lizard.

The lizard was just that and I search
uncle Google for all his names including the latinate

because poetry likes it. I want to call his belly terra-
cotta but I call it deep red ochre instead.

There it is: *Intellagama lesueurii*, meaning 'intelligent
lizard'. How about that!?

The Greatest Poem in the World

O! mighty Turkey
of the Brush. I'm sure I know
your face. Creation Being, twice now
our paths cross.

I fell in deprecation,
spoke in tongue and gobbledygook
for you. I shooed the cat gods
and gave the bird

to my neighbour. I declared
ketchup and mustard
as my totems when once-
upon-a-time I'd say nothing!

O! mighty Turkey
moving mountains with
your strut. Here now, again
I'm your egg buried in a mound.

Uninitiation

to the hum of a subaru 4×4
they invent an escape

the uncles have it all planned
criss-crossing old lines
where that big serpent story
slithers west

a comic opera of black men
a wallaby and a brolga
and a boy emu dulled
with a too-long-in-the-colony look
follow highway lined scar
trees deep into sky country

from the back seat
boy takes in the mono-crop patchwork
picture-view flickering fields
weeping weeds of paterson's curse
black dirt to red dirt
little dust devils curl their grins
in the tailwind

unc brolga notes how mulga
gently lifts from the horizon
a trick of that warm seasonal air
and begins a belly-song
navigating toward his mother's totem
eagle-hawks circling

in silent accompaniment
boy emu commits the rocky contours
of melody to memory

they find a place to camp
cut wood for the inner circle
for carving boy's first war-bundi

with his cryptid-tongue
unc wallaby
tells a tenuous fable

of those petrified great heroes
and villains painted ignobly
into landscape
as archetype
of reconciled australia
as blue
in a seafoam girt
for what
all to crack open in
the few biomes left looking
for a composer-in-residence

a whittled boy
young and free
strung with another's culture
begins to see the ground
beneath him
covered with axe heads
sees the scabs of a mulga riot
overflowing ruins

hears the hidden accents
inscribed in homelands he always knew

evening edges them fireside
quiet boy emu
uncle wallaby and brolga
lick into shape
clubs made from gidge
sounds of metal on wood
fill the nocturnal ethers

uncles leave
their dreamcraft unfinished
tell him the rest of the story-pattern
can be found in the stars
and tomorrow…

Dreams in a Language

A poem can begin
with a lie (Adrienne Rich)

and aunty B says
there is friction

in the space
between the shadow

lines of earth and sky
my peers cite

fevered futurism as if
from a bad dream

I try to write you
down, familiar,

a bream, splinter of mercury,
that evades the spear

a conversation begins
with a lie (aunty Adrienne again)

you can't be delivered
and, maybe I'm just the lure,

fretting? How can I explain?
that we still have each other

hunting real bunyips
in fictional nations.

Losing a Love Language and a Brother

Love is your name
but I leave unspoken; you know
I loved you to the roots.

You fly half-masked in
photographs, your academic
gown, your footy uniform

this crowning regalia—
You are a spectator
sport. They planted a native

tree, a namesake sandstone
library, a tennis court on sacred dirt.
I can only think of our pillow

talk. Naked, beside my naked
self on a bed of sovereign

grasses. Scholarship boys.
Cultured men. Brothers in arms.
You taught me to lingo

and I recited those places
until they left lip-shaped-scars
across the acres of your chest.

Then, someone came and
boxed your head in. Out bled

a dead language

A grammar and spelling
with a mission. Your shadow
coagulates primarily in English

best suited for obituaries
and poetry competitions.

Authority of Creeks

I adore
my sister's sons & this
tributary crow town laughter
of industry rhythm streams
flow from dense seedbank sky-
corridor to ward ancient economies
precious Gadigal way
Bidjigal pockets they're listening
to she-oak Wangal
voices regrowing yarns
on occupied land stored and spun
along this Wolli valley walk sustaining
familial inflections accents rusted
auto-orchestrations once
a chain of mobile ponds &
from their broken long before
so far from homelands
croaking english grew
cliff face caves filled
fossil flood waters with broken glass
wetland salt marsh counterparts
exhaling pan-greenery & a wound
a cadenza remnant filled this shady patch
healing topsoil
tears their properly good
ol' holiday grassroot voices
all day sing memory's out landish
creek covered ruins
in love & war

with every light-speckled lizard
sipping grevillea dew or whispers of
some such incident where new growth leaves
sunny pollen on their faces that would babble like
the Country mind & spring breezes
an image a shady
grove pooled lowest point
a story black magic
(colocasia esculenta)
stemlets tilt &
dance animate in joyful
tangles

Bay Area Studies Abroad

A psychedelic Dreamtime under Golden Gate, I'm holding his *Howl*.

Streetlight, moonlight, June town gloom, Ohlone bones ground to a fine powder.

Cinematically, the hero's tale begins on American soil.

Smoking a cigarette, nothing but a trail of tears to light the way.

Bleeding rainbows, foreign queer contemplates the big annihilation.

Oh, how many poets does it take to install a revolution?

Satire, Satyr, Sartre, Suasarre, Sunday morn diner decompression

California, invasive eucalyptus falls on man hiking.

Neon and Spice, sucking cocktails from Castro to Chinatown sidewalk.

Hitching segway rides with a Walt Whitman look-alike who gives sex tours.

I invent the first Koala Kabbalah at the human-like zoo.

Once Upon A Billabong Puddle

hot pressed open air sky brewing suspended
starstrings unwind their electric light as we stand
ankle deep in tears in earth rot and leaf mush
our clapsticks striking longtime synchronous
breaths ripple and the malaluaca councils shudder
ground and water sweeping moon eyed clearness
we take our bow to mend this hallowed meeting
place seeking alluvium solutions sip underflows
and quenching the throat with song old as ice
ages erupt for the fish gods mercurial ephemera
bubbling free bodied enlivened we tread water
head above the deep green sub-heavens and bask
in our own power

Water Ways

1.

inhale   mudflat & fennel   musk drifting
across   egret-spotted   wetland   saltmarsh

the sulphur   crested caress   of midsummer
afternoon   blankets   black ducks   as they plan

their pidgin-tongued   revolutions   and I hunger
for the rust   coloured   figs of my   youth

miss that bluetongue   who visits   weekends
& cloud   watching   with cousins   until dusk

2.

us feral kids
    squawking at shore
sticky with bubble

o' bills paddle
    pops dripping
we spot him

see his snorkel
bob in the glassy
botany

bay waters
            dad as I remember
all morning fishing

breaches the sea foam
            bare chested
and majestic

slung hand-spear
and net
his hearty bounty

onto craggy
            rockwall breakers
we kick-off

lickety-split
            bounding boulder
to boulder

like we hit
            the sky
skipping   over razor

lipped mollusc
            to meet him
to ogle fascinated

at his knife finesse
            scattering opalescent
scales

and oily
entrails
for the gulls

Transit of Venus #7

I shall conclude the account
of this Country with a few words
on the Currents and Tides:

Transit of Venus #8

I went in search of Fresh Water,
    This inlet,
but had no better success than before;
    I have named Thirsty Sound,
wherefore I gave over all thoughts, laying
    by reason we could find now…
Ship a Shore.

Transit of Venus #9

The Natives are no less plenty about the head.
We saw their faces and bodies
painted with a sort of white paint Pigment.

Seeing no stored provisions, we believe they depend
upon the present day for their subsistence.
The Natives are no less plenty about the head.

However, we could know but very little
of their customs as we never were
painted with a sort of white paint Pigment

or able to form any connections with them.
They had not so much as touch'd the stores we left.
The Natives are no less plenty about the head.

The strings of beeds we had left with
the children were found laying in the hut
painted with a sort of white paint Pigment.

We saw foot steps of Men, holes dug
in the sand. I did not wait to examine them.
The Natives are no less plenty about the head
painted with a sort of white paint Pigment.

Notes

The poems 'Dreaming Inside Dillwynia Women's Prison', 'Tiddas', 'Under Wiradjuri Sky', 'After Big Rain', 'UnLoreful', and 'Cento – They come to our house' were written after Ngana Baranagarai Workshops at various correctional facilities and juvenile detention centres across NSW. Lines from 'Cento – They come to our house' are drawn from *Scribbly Gums and Blossoms: Young People Dreaming Inside*, an anthology developed through the Ngana Barangarai program.

The 'Transit of Venus' poems use lines sourced from the diaries of James Cook. 'The Informants' uses material from Threlkeld's dictionary and his Gospel of Luke translation. 'Old Man Banksia' contains lines from Joseph Banks' diary.

'Dreams in a Language' uses lines from Adrienne Rich's 'Cartographies of Silence' from *The Dream of a Common Language: Poems 1974–1977* (W. W. Norton, 1978). All relevant permissions have been obtained for the reproduction of this material.

Acknowledgements

to lands where these poems grew: Gadigal, the Kulin Nations, Wodi Wodi, Murrawarri, Tharawal, Darug, Awabakal, Darkinjung, Wiradjuri, Gamilaroi

to all the uncles and aunties, Elders and knowledge-holders—thank you for your guidance, stories and presence throughout

to the journals publishing poems found in this collection, including *Cordite Poetry Review*, *Plumwood Mountain*, *Rabbit: A Journal for Nonfiction Poetry*, *Running Dog*, *The Suburban Review*, the *Australian Poetry Journal*, *Openbook*, and through *Red Room Poetry*; and in the anthologies *Fire Front: First Nations Poetry and Power Today*, *Active Aesthetics: Contemporary Australian Poetry*, *Nangamay Mana Djurali: First Nations LGBTQIA+ Poetry*, *Dreaming Inside*, *Sista's Green Sea Dreaming*, *Tell Me Like You Mean It*, and *Best of Australian Poems* (2021 and 2023)

to those who've shown me poetry and love go hand in hand: Aunty Barb Nicholson, Felicity Plunkett, Toby Fitch, Jazz Money

to Varuna Writers House, to the Wheeler Centre, and the Emerging Writers Festival

to Alison Whitaker, Evelyn Araluen, Lorna Munro, thanks for the invite

to folks at Magabala. I'm certain our stories have entwined for a little bit long-time deep-time to all my peers singing us on into the fields of possibility called Country

to the eagle, the spider, the moth, the snake, the stone, the fern, and ants that take my toenails before winter

to my love, my partner-in-dreaming, Grant

to my family, may we thrive on

About the author

Luke Patterson is a Gamilaroi poet, musician and educator living on Gadigal land. His work has been published in journals and anthologies nationwide. Luke's research and creative pursuits are grounded in extensive work with First Nations and other community-based organisations across Australia.

MORE TITLES FROM MAGABALA BOOKS

FALSE
CLAIMS OF
COLONIAL
THIEVES
CHARMAINE
PAPERTALK GREEN
& JOHN KINSELLA

KINDRED
KIRLI SAUNDERS
2020
ABIA
AUSTRALIAN BOOK INDUSTRY AWARDS
SHORTLISTED
Victorian Premier's Literary Awards 2021
Shortlist

Woven

First Nations poetic conversations from the Fair Trade project

Commissioned by Red Room Poetry

Edited by Anne-Marie Te Whiu

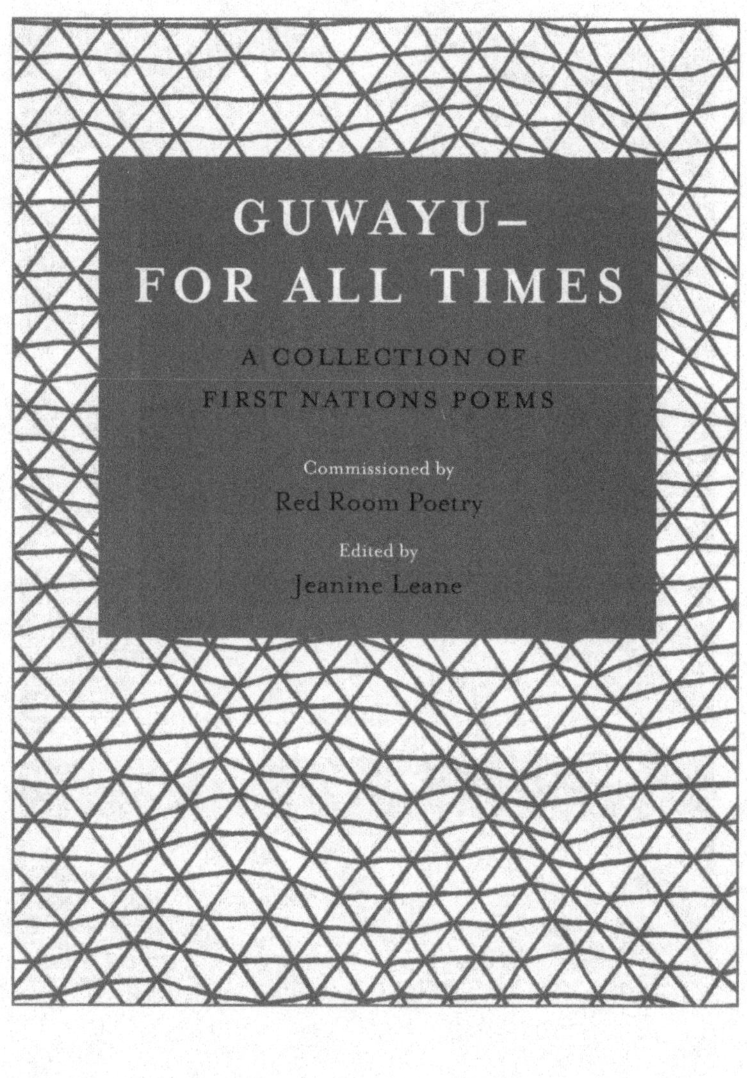
GUWAYU–
FOR ALL TIMES
A COLLECTION OF
FIRST NATIONS POEMS
Commissioned by
Red Room Poetry
Edited by
Jeanine Leane